P9-CBE-290

A king for Israel

Story by Penny Frank

Illustrated by Tony Morris

THE LION
STORY BIBLE

17

TRING · BATAVIA · SYDNEY

The Bible tells us
how God chose the Israelites to be his
special people. He made them a
promise that he would always love
and care for them. But they must
obey him.

This is the second part of the story
of the prophet Samuel. You can find
the story in your own Bible, in the
first book of Samuel, chapters 8 to 15.

Copyright © 1986 Lion Publishing

Published by
Lion Publishing plc
Icknield Way, Tring, Herts, England
ISBN 0 85648 742 2
Lion Publishing Corporation
1705 Hubbard Avenue, Batavia,
Illinois 60510, USA
ISBN 0 85648 742 2
Albatross Books Pty Ltd
PO Box 320, Sutherland, NSW 2232, Australia
ISBN 0 86760 526 X

First edition 1986
Reprinted 1987

All rights reserved

Printed and bound in Hong Kong

**British Library Cataloguing in
Publication Data**

Frank, Penny
   A king for Israel. – (The Lion Story
Bible; 17)
1. Samuel – Juvenile literature
I. Title   II. Morris, Tony
222'.40924   BS580.S5

ISBN 0-85648-742-2

**Library of Congress Cataloging in
Publication Data**

Frank, Penny.
   A king for Israel.
(The Lion Story Bible; 17)
1. Samuel (Biblical judge) – Juvenile
literature.
2. Bible. O.T. – Biography – Juvenile
literature.
[1. Saul, King of Israel. 2. Samuel
(Biblical judge). 3. Bible – O.T.]
I. Morris, Tony, ill. II. Title. III. Series:
Frank, Penny. Lion Story Bible; 17.
BS580.S2F69 1986   222'.4309505
85-13118
ISBN 0-85648-742-2

Samuel had been a priest in God's temple for a long time. He was a good man. But now he was old, and the Israelites would soon need a new leader.

The Israelites were jealous of the people
in the lands nearby because they had a
king to lead them.

   'We want a king too,' the Israelites told
Samuel. 'He will rule us and lead us in
battle.'

Samuel talked to God about what the
people had said.

'But I am their King,' God said to
Samuel. 'I want them to serve me and
I will take care of them.'

When Samuel told the people, they
said, 'Oh no. We want a real king,
like everyone else.'

'The people will not listen to me,' God said. 'So I will give them the king they want, even though it will mean trouble.'

Samuel did not know where to start
looking for a king. But he trusted God
to show him the right man.

Now in a place called Ephraim there
was an Israelite called Kish. He was
a rich man. Everyone knew him.

Kish had a tall, good-looking son
called Saul.

One day Kish found that some of his
donkeys were missing.

'You will have to go to find them,'
Kish told Saul. So Saul set off with
a servant to look for the donkeys.

Saul and his servant walked a long way over the hills. They asked all the people they met, 'Have you seen our donkeys? We have lost them.'

But no one had seen the donkeys.

They came to a town. Saul said, 'We won't find our donkeys in the town! We'd better go home. My father will be worried.'

But the servant knew that Samuel was in the town.

'Let's ask Samuel,' he said to Saul. 'He knows everything.'

God spoke to Samuel as Saul came along the road.

'That young man's name is Saul,' said God. 'You must make him the first king of Israel.'

So Samuel asked the two men to come
into the house and rest.

'Don't worry about the donkeys,' he
told them. 'They have been found
already.'

The two men were very surprised.
They had not told Samuel they were
looking for the donkeys.

14

Samuel looked at Saul as he came into the house. He saw how tall and strong he was.

'The people will be glad to have such a handsome king,' he thought.

They sat down to have a good meal together. Samuel treated Saul as a special visitor.

Early in the morning Samuel woke up
the two men and took them to the road
out of the town.

'I have a secret to tell you,' he said to
Saul. The other man went on, so that he
would not hear.

'God has chosen you to be a king of Israel,' Samuel told Saul.

Samuel poured some oil over Saul's head. Saul knew it was the way of showing that God had chosen him.

Then Saul went home. But he kept the secret Samuel had told him.

Not long after, Samuel called the Israelites together. Saul was there with everyone else.

'Here is the man God has chosen to be your king,' he said. And Saul stood up, tall and handsome.

The Israelites were very glad. Now they would be like the other people who lived near them.

'Long live the king!' they shouted.

So now, when the Israelites had wars,
King Saul led the soldiers into battle.
The people were very proud of their tall,
strong king.

Their enemies were afraid to fight
them. They knew what a good king Saul
was.

At first all went well, but as time went by Saul grew proud. He forgot to obey God.

He did not listen to what Samuel said, so the Israelites forgot to serve God too.

One day King Saul's army fought the Amalekites. After the battle, King Saul and his army took some of the good things the Amalekites had owned. But God had told them to take nothing.

Samuel said to Saul, 'You have disobeyed God. And God is sorry he made you king. One day he will choose someone else.'

Not long after, God said to Samuel, 'Saul will not be king for ever! It is time to tell the new king of my plans.'

So Samuel set out for Bethlehem. God
had sent him to find one of the sons of
a man called Jesse. Samuel did not know
it yet, but the new king's name was
David.

The Lion Story Bible is made up of 52 individual stories for young readers, building up an understanding of the Bible as one story — God's story — a story for all time and all people.

The Old Testament section (numbers 1–30) tells the story of a great nation — God's chosen people, the Israelites — and God's love and care for them through good times and bad. The stories are about people who knew and trusted God. From this nation came one special person, Jesus Christ, sent by God to save all people everywhere.

The story of Israel's first king comes from the Old Testament, 1 Samuel, chapters 8–15.

God did not want his people to have a king. He was their King. He wanted them to depend on him. But the nations around all had kings, and the Israelites wanted a king to protect them and lead them in battle.

Through the prophet Samuel, God warned his people that a king would give them trouble and hardship. But they would not listen. And so God gave them what they asked.

He chose Saul. At first all went well. But soon his new power went to Saul's head. He disobeyed God, and his disobedience brought trouble.

The next story in this series, number 18: *David and Goliath*, is one of the most famous Bible stories of all.